in the news™

INCARCERATION IN AMERICA

Kerry Hinton

ROSEN
PUBLISHING®

New York

Published in 2010 by The Rosen Publishing Group, Inc.
29 East 21st Street, New York, NY 10010

Copyright © 2010 by The Rosen Publishing Group, Inc.

First Edition

Library of Congress Cataloging-in-Publication Data

Hinton, Kerry.
Incarceration in America / Kerry Hinton. — 1st ed.
    p. cm. — (In the news)
Includes bibliographical references and index.
ISBN-13: 978-1-4358-5277-8 (library binding)
ISBN-13: 978-1-4358-5560-1 (pbk)
ISBN-13: 978-1-4358-5561-8 (6 pack)
1. Prisons — United States. 2. Imprisonment — United States. I. Title.
HV9471.H56 2010
365'.973 — dc22

2008046969

Manufactured in the United States of America

On the cover: Clockwise, from upper left: part of a prison cell block; department of corrections officers; supplemental living quarters, Mule Creek State Prison, California.

contents

Many Prisons, Many Problems

merica's criminal justice system is facing a crisis. There are more people in U.S. prisons and jails than ever before. With more prisons in operation than any other country in the world, the United States is in the midst of a situation that will not improve without real and serious change.

Today's prisons have become breeding grounds for violence, drug abuse, mental illness, and the spread of infectious diseases. Excessive overcrowding in prisons only makes these problems worse. According to the U.S. Department of Justice, more than 2.3 million men and women are currently serving sentences in federal prisons, state prisons, and local jails. Considering the population of our country (approximately 305 million at the end of 2008), this seems to be a low number. However, China has a population of 1.3 billion—almost five times that of the United States—and there are only 1.6 million men and women incarcerated in the Chinese penal system. A 2007 report by the Pew Center states that 1 in every 99.1 American citizens is in prison. If there are any doubts that our prison system is in dire need of change, then these figures should remove them.

There is a clear relationship between poverty and incarceration. People living under economic stress have less opportunity to obtain the education and skills needed to pursue gainful employment. People living in poverty are much more likely to spend time in jail or prison than people living more comfortably. Poorer families often have less time to spend with their children, which may lead to an increase in juvenile offenses. Poverty creates a vicious cycle, as juvenile offenders are more likely to return to the criminal justice system as adults.

Certainly, prisons are necessary—all Americans have the right to live safely in their communities. On the other hand, imprisonment should not be viewed as a cure for criminal behavior. In some cases, a prison sentence may not be the best way to prevent further crimes or rehabilitate criminals. Life in prison is by no means designed to be a pleasant experience. However, the lives that many inmates live behind bars do them little good once they are set to rejoin society. Some leave prison with worse habits and behavior than before they entered. For them, prison time can almost be viewed as "criminal college." With more than five thousand prisons and jails in operation today, millions of inmates leave the penal system each year. For their sake, and for society's sake, they must leave better equipped to interact with society at large than before they entered.

All of these issues raise a larger question: Do our penitentiaries work? In the eyes of many, the answer is no. Huge prison budgets, poor medical care, inadequate educational opportunities, and increasing violence all present challenges to our prison system.

The Purpose of Prisons

Why do we need prisons, jails, and penitentiaries? What is life like inside prison? What is being done to improve the prison system in the United States? If the answers to these and more questions interest you, then this book will provide you with plenty of information and resources. A good place to start is with the definition of incarceration. To incarcerate means "to put in prison." The purpose of incarceration, according to criminologist Dr. Alfred J. Blumstein, is two-fold: punishment and crime control. These goals can be reached in one of three ways:

Incapacitation
Incarcerating people to prevent them from committing crimes is called incapacitation. Incapacitation often involves a set minimum sentence for certain crimes. On the other hand, incapacitation may require longer

sentences for people who present a greater risk for repeating a crime.

Deterrence

Deterrence is closely linked to incapacitation. To deter is to prevent. Imprisoning criminals says to the public that criminal behavior will not be tolerated. It also raises awareness of penalties for criminal acts.

Rehabilitation

Rehabilitation is the attempt to reform an individual and correct bad behavior. (A shortened version, "rehab," may be familiar from television and news programs.) In the world of criminal justice, prisoner rehabilitation typically involves education, discipline, and treatment for drug addictions or mental diseases.

Incarceration: A Brief History

While prisons have existed since the days of ancient Greece, the prisons of today are quite different. Before the fifteenth century, lawbreakers spent less time in confinement. In most cases, people suspected of wrongdoing were held while awaiting trial, punishment, or execution. Punishments meted out after trial rarely involved further prison time and ranged from flogging

A fourteenth-century mosaic in Florence, Italy, depicts a prisoner being thrown into jail.

(beatings) to death. The conditions of imprisonment were much worse than those found in today's prisons. Local authorities did not supply many comforts to prisoners, leaving family and friends to supply necessities like food and medicine. Living conditions were dark and damp, and there was no heat or proper disposal for human waste.

By the fifteenth century, prisons in medieval Europe began to look a little more like the facilities that are familiar to us today. However, prison holding spaces were still tight, damp, and unsanitary. This led to poor health and death for many inmates. Prisoner health and welfare remained a low priority until the Penitentiary Act of 1779 was passed in England. This law required prisons to provide food and clothing, as well as private rooms known as cells. Supporters of this law hoped that better conditions and hard work could help rehabilitate criminals.

Prisons in America

Early prisons in America borrowed from the laws and institutions of England. One of the first prisons in America to use the English ideas of criminal rehabilitation was the Walnut Street Jail in Philadelphia, Pennsylvania. After it was begun, in 1773, conditions at Walnut Street were atrocious. Then, a group of prominent citizens organized for improved conditions in Pennsylvania's prisons, using Walnut Street as a model. By 1790, conditions there were much better than in other American prisons, and inmates were offered education and religious study to help them see the error of their ways.

In 1816, the most modern prison up to that time was in Auburn, New York. Auburn State Penitentiary was built differently than other prisons. It had multiple levels, with cells that guards could observe at the same time. Many aspects of modern prisons were developed at Auburn. These include prison labor and communal dining (a large number of prisoners eating together). Over the next one hundred years, many prisons opened across the United States using Auburn as a model.

In the twentieth century, new prisons expanded on the ideas of Auburn. To improve rehabilitation, more penitentiaries began to provide inmates with classroom education, job training, and counseling. These remain features of U.S. prison life today.

Alternatives to Imprisonment

In addition to incarceration, there are many other ways of dealing with lawbreakers. These alternative ideas have been around as long as prisons. Early alternatives included fines, community service, and conscription (forced military service). Later alternatives to incarceration included various treatment programs.

Prison alternatives have become a hot topic in recent years. One of the biggest reasons for this development is the drug policy in the United States. Instead of reducing drug dealing and use, the most visible result of the U.S. government's war on drugs has been dangerous overcrowding in the prison system. More than twenty years after the strict antidrug laws of the 1980s, it has become clear that imprisonment alone does not solve the problems of drug-related crimes. More money than ever before, both public and private, is being spent to house, feed, and provide medical care to low-risk inmates. For drug offenders, alternatives to imprisonment make better financial sense.

Most advocates agree that prison alternatives should be aimed at nonviolent offenders. For them, education, drug treatment, and counseling are believed to be more appropriate and enlightened methods of assistance. The following are some common alternatives to long-term imprisonment:

Boot Camps

Boot camps are used to prevent young offenders from committing crimes and returning to prison in their adult years. Attendance is often ordered by a judge as a sentence and can last from three to six months. Boot camps for juveniles are modeled after boot camps for armed forces enlistees. Life in juvenile boot camps includes intense discipline and physical activity.

Opponents of these programs point to the case of fourteen-year-old Martin Lee Anderson. Less than a day after his arrival at a Florida juvenile boot camp, Anderson collapsed in the exercise yard. Security camera footage showed him being forced to breathe in ammonia fumes in an attempt to revive him. Later, Anderson's limp body was shown being manhandled by camp guards. Boot

Instead of serving prison time, juvenile offenders in boot camps work on their physical and mental discipline.

camps were developed as an alternative to the violent culture of adult prisons. Anderson's death sparked a reevaluation of boot camps for young offenders.

Probation

People sentenced to probation do not serve prison sentences. Their sentences are set aside as long as they do not violate the terms set down by the sentencing judge. In some cases, criminals may be ordered not to travel, to pay a fine, or to attend regular meetings with a counselor or probation officer. Probation is generally not a suitable option for violent offenders.

Diversion

This alternative diverts, or moves, first-time offenders out of the penal system and into more appropriate institutions, such as drug or alcohol treatment centers. When combined with probation, diversion can be very effective at rehabilitating offenders. In some states, completing a diversion program can erase a conviction from someone's criminal record.

Teaching

Instead of jail time, criminals with college degrees may be allowed to teach prison inmates or give lectures to juvenile offenders about their experiences with the law. This prison alternative provides inmates with valuable knowledge that they can use once they are released.

Work Release

This is different from work release for prison inmates, which will be discussed in chapter 3. As an alternative to incarceration, work release is a type of probation in which the offender is sentenced to work a particular job, usually in the community. People sentenced to work-release programs are allowed to stay in their homes at night. Lateness or absences can sometimes

Celebrity Martha Stewart displays an electronic monitoring anklet. She was required to wear it as part of a home-confinement sentence.

end the work release and result in prison or jail time.

House Arrest

House arrest is more severe than the alternatives mentioned above. Criminals under house arrest are confined to their homes for the duration of their sentences. Some offenders may be ordered to wear electronic monitoring devices that notify police if they have gone beyond a certain distance from their home. Violating house arrest can result in prison and jail time.

The alternate types of punishment mentioned above are already being used across the nation. Expanding them could free up billions of federal tax dollars that are currently spent on a prison system that does not fully meet the goals of incarceration.

Prison Types and Conditions

Are prisons and jails the same? In some countries, the answer is yes. But in the United States, they are quite different. The easiest way to tell the difference between prisons and jails is by measuring the amount of time that inmates spend in each.

Jails are normally intended to house people for one year or less. Local governments (counties or cities) are responsible for running them. Jails hold prisoners who have committed crimes in other states or counties, people who have violated parole, and other short-term detainees. Jails are smaller than prisons and do not have some of the facilities that are found at prisons. Since most jail inmates are not staying for long, jails do not have exercise areas or doctors, except for emergencies. One exception is Rikers Island, a collection of New York City jails (also known as a penal colony). Rikers includes ten separate jails, a bakery, and even its own power plant.

Prisons may be managed by states or, at the federal level, by the U.S. government. Prisons hold inmates

This is a cell block within the U.S. penitentiary at Marion, Illinois.

for longer periods than jails. State or federal prisons offer medical and dental appointments, psychological counseling, and exercise. In short, prisons deal with a greater number of inmates. And they have more space, more services—and more problems.

From Crime to Incarceration

A person is not sent to jail or prison unless he or she has been found guilty of a crime. Sometimes, if the evidence against the person is very strong, then the accused pleads guilty. More often, a guilty plea is the result of a plea bargain. This means the accused admits his or her guilt in exchange for less jail time. Plea bargains may be used as negotiating tools.

For the accused, plea bargaining is often a better option than risking a maximum sentence if a guilty verdict is reached at trial. "Copping" (or accepting) a plea may also result in a lesser charge. For instance, a burglary charge may be reduced to attempted burglary. Almost 90 percent of all criminal cases in the United States are resolved through plea bargaining.

If the accused pleads innocent, then he or she will have to appear at trial. At trial, a jury views evidence and decides the defendant's guilt or innocence. A verdict of "not guilty" results in an acquittal for the accused. The accused is then free to go without any penalties. If the verdict is "guilty," then the judge will decide how much time the convicted must spend behind bars and in what type of prison the sentence will be served.

Some crimes require a minimum sentence. This means a judge is forced to deliver a fixed sentence to any individual convicted of the crime. Michigan's 650-Lifer Law, for example, requires a minimum sentence of twenty years for anyone making, selling, or possessing more than 650 grams (about 23 ounces) of cocaine or similar drugs. Such laws provide a heavy penalty to discourage people from breaking them.

In cases where minimum sentencing is not required, judges decide the length of prison sentences. Judges carefully consider many factors, including the circumstances of the crime, the type of crime, and the criminal record of the offender. Someone who has never been convicted of a crime may receive a lesser sentence than someone who has broken laws repeatedly. Along with sentence length, judges also decide where convicted criminals will serve their time.

Sentence length can sometimes be shortened. Some inmates are awarded time off their sentences for good behavior or service while in jail. After serving the minimum sentence, some inmates may be eligible to appear in front of a parole board. A parole board looks at an inmate's record and evaluates various factors, including his or her behavior while incarcerated. The board then decides if that person is ready to rejoin society. In the last twenty years, parole has become very rare. As of 2008, it is available only to those incarcerated in some state prisons and to federal prisoners convicted before November 1, 1987.

If a person who is declared guilty maintains his or her innocence, then that person has the right to appeal. This allows for a case to be reheard by the court that originally handed down the sentence. If more evidence has been discovered following sentencing, or certain evidence was not heard at trial, then the convicted can

A murder suspect (*left*) discusses trial matters with the presiding judge.

appeal a case to a higher court. Even after a sentence has begun, an inmate still has the opportunity to appeal. Although many appeals are denied, the right to appeal is crucial to our justice system.

Different Laws, Different Prisons

In the United States, there are two types of laws: state and federal. Individuals who break state criminal laws serve their sentences in state prisons. Violators of federal criminal laws are sent to federal prisons.

Many federal and state laws are similar, but federal laws normally have priority. The U.S. Constitution allows states to govern themselves, but the federal government will often step in when crimes are committed that may involve more complicated cases—a crime that crosses state lines, for example. Criminals arrested by federal organizations like the Federal Bureau of Investigation (FBI) are usually subject to federal laws, trials, and prisons. As of 2008, there are more than one hundred federal prisons.

Levels of Security

Prisons are classified according to levels of security. The greater the risk a prisoner poses to society, the higher the security level. The number and name of levels vary from state to state, but the restrictions prisoners face are the same. The U.S. Bureau of Prisons uses the following security classifications:

Minimum Security

This is the lowest level of prison security. Convicted felons who pose a low risk of escape or have minimal behavior problems will be housed in minimum-security facilities. Such felons include first-time, nonviolent offenders and prisoners at the end of their sentences who are awaiting release from prisons with higher security levels. Inmates here sleep in dormitories that

This is a building on the grounds of the minimum-security Alderson Federal Prison Camp, in Alderson, West Virginia.

contain many beds and shared bathrooms. Guards are present but are generally not armed, especially if the prison is in a remote area. Most minimum-security prisoners have not committed violent crimes, and many spend their sentences working under supervision for a nearby community or larger prison. These facilities are also known as federal prison camps (FPCs).

Low Security

This is a federal correctional institution (FCI). This level is similar to minimum security, but it includes additional security features to go along with increased prisoner risk. Low-security prisons have well-defined and patrolled perimeters, or boundaries, and double fencing. There are more guards per prisoner as well.

Medium Security

One in every four prisons is a medium-security FCI. These prisons have a much more intense level of control over inmates. Instead of dormitory-style housing, most inmates are kept in traditional jail cells, usually with a cellmate. Visits from the outside world are much more restricted than at prisons with lower security measures. These prisons hold violent, as well as nonviolent, prisoners. Many city and county jails keep inmates under this type of security.

High or Maximum Security

Fifteen percent of U.S. prisons are maximum security. Prisoners in these facilities have very restricted freedom. All inmates have their own cells and are monitored around the clock by armed guards and security cameras. Cell doors are controlled remotely, and guards always escort prisoners anytime they leave the cellblock, which is rarely. Some maximum-security prisons allow inmates out of their cells for only one hour per day. Maximum-security prisons are surrounded by high fences, often topped with razor wire, and may use guard dogs to deter escape on the prison grounds. Many prisons have guard towers outside as well, which are manned by armed guards to prevent escape attempts.

Supermax

This is the highest possible level of security and confinement in federal and state prisons. Supermax (super maximum) prisons are dedicated to the confinement of the most danger-ous prisoners. These include inmates who have committed serious violent crimes (murder-ers, rapists), prisoners who are

Guard towers help prevent escapes at high-security prisons.

very likely to try to escape, and those convicted of spying against the United States. Supermax prisoners live and eat in solitary confinement. They are briefly allowed out of their cells once a day, and they are allowed out-of-doors once a week. In many supermax units, furniture is made of concrete to prevent inmates from using parts to make weapons. Some prisons have supermax wings along with medium- and maximum-security areas.

Administrative Security

According to the Bureau of Prisons, these are prisons that have "special missions." They may include prisons that provide care for inmates with serious medical conditions (Medical Care for Federal Prisoners, or MCFP prisons) to supermax (ADX) prisons. Most state prison systems do not have separate administrative security facilities, but they do have units within their systems that serve the same purpose.

The more dangerous or violent a prisoner is, the fewer privileges he or she has. For instance, medium-security prisons offer some prisoners the chance to receive education toward a high school diploma. Supermax prisoners are denied that opportunity.

Women's Prisons

Most women convicted of crimes in the United States serve their sentences in female-only facilities. The structure, security level, and daily routine are virtually the same as in men's prisons. A small number of women will stay in coed prisons, which house both men and women. The two groups share educational classes, as well as dining and exercise facilities. Coed prisons often have both male and female guards watching over inmates.

Between the Bars: Prison Life

Many factors determine the day-to-day life of an inmate. Among the most important are prison type (federal or state), location, and security level. Different states have different rules regarding prisoners' privileges and daily routines.

Prison Staff

The prison staff is in charge of daily operations. There are usually two levels of staff: wardens and correctional officers.

Prison Wardens

Prison wardens can be compared to police chiefs or school principals. Many are appointed by state governors and are responsible for the day-to-day management of all levels of prisons. Wardens may also be called administrators or superintendents. Prison wardens oversee correctional officers, medical staff, and all other

A correctional officer escorts a group of inmates through the Deuel Vocational Institute in Tracy, California.

prison employees. In addition, they control the prison budget, which is the money the prison has to operate.

Correctional Officers

Correctional officers, or prison guards, are responsible for maintaining order inside prison walls and making sure rules and schedules are followed. They are also the first line of defense in case of fires, riots, or hostage situations. As security levels rise, so do the threats of danger to the correctional officers. The chance of a low-security correctional officer facing a full-scale riot is much less than it is for an officer at a maximum-security prison. Correctional officers are expected to undergo extensive training in lethal (deadly) and nonlethal weapons, first aid, self-defense, and the use of force.

Prison Routine

Routine is very important inside of a prison. Wardens and guards do their best to make sure that inmates stay on schedule. Strict timetables and discipline play big roles in the punishment of incarceration.

A prison's security level determines inmate schedules. Inmates in minimum- or low-security prisons are allowed more freedoms than inmates in facilities with tighter security. No matter what the security level, however, prison days begin at an early hour. Inmates wake up and are usually counted once before breakfast. Head counts are a constant reminder to prisoners that they are no longer a part of free society. Most prisons have at least three head counts daily for accountability and discipline.

In lower-security prisons, inmates spend their morning hours involved in school classes or work details. Basic prison work can include kitchen duties, laundry detail, maintenance, and clerical (office) jobs. Some work details leave the prison to perform maintenance or cleanup of highways, roads, or other public spaces. Prisoners are normally given time for exercise at some point during the day, for one to two hours.

Lunch, like breakfast, is not a leisurely affair. Inmates usually have about a half hour to eat before they return to their jobs. After work and before dinner, another head count is taken. After their evening meal, inmates have some free time to use telephones, read, or watch television. At least one more head count is taken before the lights are turned out, which usually occurs between

11 PM and 12 AM. This cycle restarts six to eight hours later for the duration of an inmate's sentence.

Many maximum-security prisons have only meals and head counts in common with lower-security penitentiaries. Inmates in these prisons spend much more time isolated in their cells, and they take their meals alone.

Prison Industry: Employment Behind Bars

Aside from the basic maintenance and kitchen duties prisoners perform, some inmates are required to work for pay in all federal and some state prisons. About one-fifth of inmates work in a prison industry. They often make products for purchase and use outside prison walls, such as clothes, military helmets, stereo speakers, paintbrushes, and airplane parts.

Inmates can earn from twelve cents an hour to minimum wage, about $6.55 per hour. Many learn valuable skills for use after their release. Federal prisoners who owe money for child support or legal fees must give 50 percent of their income to repay these and other debts. Research indicates that inmates who work while imprisoned are less likely to return to prison than those who do not. Many people view prison employment as a privilege for inmates, rather than a punishment, as prisoners do make a salary while incarcerated. On the other hand, critics of this system note that this arrangement is similar to slave labor or the work requirements of sweatshops in poorer countries.

Prisoner Rights

The Bill of Rights is the name given to the first ten amendments of the U.S. Constitution. They protect the most basic rights that U.S. citizens have. If a person commits a crime, however, then he or she loses some of these rights. Denying prisoners certain rights is often used to keep order behind bars. As one obvious example, inmates do not have Second Amendment rights—the right to keep and bear firearms. Weapons of any kind are a serious threat to order and safety for prison staff and inmates alike.

Some rights are not completely taken away but are limited for inmates. Prisoners have the right to free speech, but they may be punished if what they say interferes with the daily routine or encourages bad behavior among the prison population. Convicted inmates also lose the right to privacy. Prison staff may search their cells and belongings at any time, looking for illegal items. These items, called contraband, include weapons and drugs. Inmates also lose their right to privacy for mail. Incoming mail is usually opened and checked for contraband.

Other prisoner rights can be lost during imprisonment and denied even after a sentence is served. For example, convicted felons lose the right to vote in elections while they are serving their sentences. A few states have laws preventing felons from voting even after their release.

Inmates do have some guaranteed rights. Fair prisoner treatment is an international concern. According to the United Nations, a worldwide organization made up of the United States and almost two hundred other countries: "All prisoners shall be treated with respect due to their inherent dignity and value as human beings." Some basic prisoner rights include food, clothing, light, and proper ventilation; access to writing materials; freedom of religion; limited personal property; access to law books; and visits from friends and family.

Muslim inmates face the holy city of Mecca and pray. Freedom of religious worship is a basic right for prisoners.

If an inmate feels that these rights have been denied by a prison or its staff, then the inmate has the right to file a lawsuit with the government to regain them. Many of these suits refer to the Eighth Amendment of the Constitution, which prohibits any punishment considered "cruel and unusual."

Privileges

The privileges we take for granted in everyday life are not enjoyed by prison inmates. The ones that are allowed depend on the location of a particular prison, as well as the prison security level. All federal prisons have the same set of rules and regulations. For state prison, privileges are decided by the individual state.

Telephone

A highly valued prison privilege is phone use. Telephone access can be used as a tool to maintain inmate order and discipline. For example, inmates in Texas state prisons who are not taking classes or working in a prison industry are denied phone use. In many other prisons, inmates have the right to use prison phones for legal purposes. But in almost all other cases, telephone use in prison is a perk, or special privilege. Some prisons have begun to allow inmates limited use of e-mail accounts in place of phone use. In prisons, phone use does not mean cellular phones, which are illegal in all state and federal penitentiaries.

Spousal Visits

In some prisons, husbands and wives of inmates are allowed to stay with their spouses in private for overnight or weekend visits. These are known as conjugal visits. They are very rare—only a few states allow them—and they are not permitted in federal prisons. Some prisons do not allow conjugal visits because they can provide the spouse of an inmate with an opportunity to smuggle in drugs or weapons.

Educational Classes

A small percentage of prisoners are allowed to take advantage of educational and vocational opportunities while in prison. Those without high school diplomas can take classes for the General Education Development (GED) test. Some prisons also provide classes offered by colleges and universities. Many prisons have vocational courses to teach inmates such skills as woodworking, welding, and computer technology. As some prisoners have never had formal education, vocational training is an important part of their rehabilitation. As with most prison privileges, only inmates with good behavior records are eligible for education or vocational benefits.

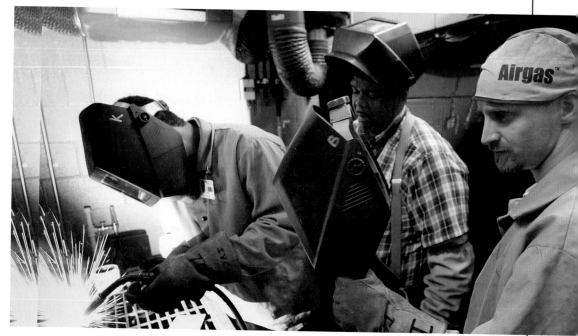

Inmates at Sheridan Correctional Institute in Illinois learn welding skills they can use after their release from prison.

Work Release and Furlough

Another rare privilege for inmates is work release. Under this program, an inmate who was employed at the time of his or her conviction can be allowed to continue working at his or her job during the day. States would rather have an inmate working and paying taxes to defray some of the cost of his or her incarceration.

The rules for work release are very strict. Inmates are escorted to the workplace and are monitored while they are at their jobs. They are not permitted to leave work, have visits, or make nonbusiness phone calls during the workday. After working hours, the inmate is required to return to prison. Violation of any of these rules can end a work-release agreement. Violent criminals are not usually approved for work-release programs.

Prison furlough is a rare privilege for inmates. It is similar to the weekend pass that soldiers and sailors receive in the military. Furloughs are sometimes used to make an inmate's return to society easier. Inmates with a very small amount of time left on their sentences (ninety days, in most cases) may be permitted to leave prison without an escort for periods ranging from twelve to seventy-two hours. Furloughs with escorts are also given in order for inmates to attend funerals, visit ill family members, and receive extended medical care.

Punishments

Discipline is necessary for any prison to run safely and smoothly. For this reason, inmates who do not obey prison rules are subject to punishment. Common punishments involve removal of the privileges discussed above. For more serious violations of prison rules, other kinds of discipline are used. Many punishments given to inmates are designed to make daily life more like that of an inmate in a higher-security prison.

Solitary confinement is a harsh punishment that some inmates receive. In prison slang, it is called "the hole." Inmates are placed in a cell and have no contact with anyone except correctional officers or medical staff. They are served meals in their cells and are allowed out of their cells for only one hour per day. Federal prisons and some states call this kind of confinement a special or security housing unit (SHU). This type of confinement is similar to the daily lives of inmates in supermax prisons.

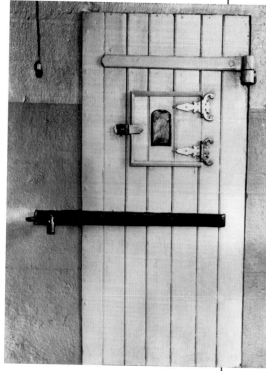

A solitary confinement cell at Joliet Correction Center is shown here circa 1936.

Inmates who are in physical danger from other prisoners may be placed in a less severe form of solitary confinement called protective custody. These inmates include witnesses to in-prison crimes, people who have committed crimes against children, and gang members. Protective custody can also be used to isolate extremely violent inmates.

In extreme situations, prison staff may have to punish a large number of inmates. This most commonly occurs when a prison is the scene of frequent, large-scale fights, or to maintain order after a riot. In these cases, a prison may go into lockdown. Prisoners in lockdown must stay in their cells or rooms, leaving only to eat or work. Lockdowns can last from a few hours to many years.

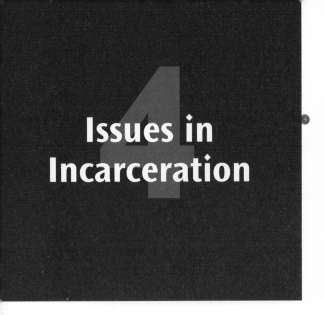

Issues in Incarceration

The problems that America's prisons are facing can bring these institutions to the brink of failure. This chapter explores some of the more serious challenges to our country's penal system.

Prison Overcrowding

Prison overcrowding is cited as the major problem in the United States. As mentioned in chapter 1, the U.S. Department of Justice reports that more than 2.3 million Americans were serving sentences in federal prisons, state prisons, and local jails as of the beginning of 2008. According to the International Center for Prison Studies at King's College London, England, the United States has more inmates per capita than any other developed country. Japan, for instance, has 83 prisoners for every 100,000 citizens. England has about 151 prisoners for every 100,000 citizens. The United States has about 762 prisoners per 100,000 citizens.

Millions of American inmates are crammed into facilities that do not have enough room to handle them. This overcrowding increases the risk of violence and increases health risks, such as the spread of diseases. Overcrowding also puts a severe financial strain on state and federal governments. The Pew Center estimates that the United States will spend an additional $27 billion before 2011 in order to cope with overly high prison populations.

This gym at California's Mule Creek Prison had to be converted into makeshift living quarters.

Stiffer Drug Laws

In 1986, Congress passed the Anti-Drug Abuse Act, which ordered mandatory minimum sentences for cocaine possession. At the time, rock cocaine, or crack, was an overwhelming problem in American cities. Crack is cheaper than powdered cocaine and is much more addictive. In the eyes of this law, the penalty for having 5 grams (about 1 teaspoon) of crack is now the same as the penalty for 500 grams (105 tsp)

Inmates share a cell at the Sheridan Correctional Center in Illinois, a facility specifically for inmates with drug and alcohol problems.

of powdered cocaine. Crack cocaine was the bane of inner-city neighborhoods, areas in which the residents are more likely to be African Americans and other minorities. Because of this, many critics say that America's federal drug laws create unfair punishment for African Americans and those of other minority groups.

If one of the goals of imprisonment is crime control, then we need to find out why drug crimes are not dropping at the same rate that drug offenders are entering prisons. Mandatory minimum drug laws may have something to do with this. According to Senator Jim Webb of Virginia, more people are being imprisoned because of stricter laws, not because there is more crime. In 2005, 4 out of 5 people in prison for drug offenses were in for possession, not sales. Rather than receiving treatment, drug users too often land in prison.

Drug Use in Prison

A prison sentence does not necessarily put an end to an inmate's drug use. Illegal drugs are a significant problem inside prisons and penitentiaries. Prison visitors are the most common smugglers of illegal drugs into state and federal prisons. According to a 2003 Associated Press article, smugglers use everything from baby diapers to burritos to get drugs inside.

Aside from visitors, drugs also enter prisons through the mail. Or, they are carried by prison staff. At the Central Oklahoma Correctional facility, for example, guards were found bringing drugs to inmates. The guards were fired, but they were not charged with any crime. This may not be the case at every prison in America, but the fact that it happens at all is noteworthy.

In some cases, inmates who have never used drugs may find them more available inside prison walls.

Placing drug offenders in treatment programs instead of in prison may help to control or lessen the amount of drugs in U.S. prisons today.

"Three Strikes" Laws

Mandatory minimum sentencing laws apply to more than drug offenses. Other examples of this type of sentencing are the so-called "three strikes" laws that almost half of the states in America have passed. Under these laws, someone convicted of a serious or violent crime for the third time receives a harsher punishment than first- or second-time offenders. In California, for example, the mandatory minimum for a third strike is twenty-five years.

Recidivism

One of the greatest problems that the criminal justice system faces is recidivism. "Recidivism" is a term used to describe when people repeat bad behavior, even after it has resulted in their punishment. Nationally, more than half of all offenders are back in prison within three years. The re-arrest rate is even higher for sex offenders. With figures like these, it is difficult to say that U.S. prisons are working as well as they should.

Why are recidivism rates so high? Most say the answer to that question is inadequate prisoner education and training. The U.S. Department of Education calls low recidivism "the ultimate measure of success" for the effectiveness of our prisons. Unfortunately, state prison budgets have been strained by yearly inmate increases, making it difficult to provide proper education to inmates. It costs more than $60 billion to incarcerate all of the inmates in this country, according to the U.S. Courts Office of Public Affairs. California spends approximately $49,000 on each inmate per year. Out of this total, almost half is spent on correctional staff and security measures. In comparison, only $600 of this total goes to educate each inmate. With so little money being spent on education, opportunities for quality training are very low for the average inmate.

Education and training are important because unless an inmate receives life in prison without the opportunity for parole, he or she will eventually reenter society. Without skills and rehabilitation, the chance of further criminal activity remains high for ex-convicts.

Youth Imprisonment

Juvenile offenders (young people who are usually between the ages of seven and eighteen) have their own courts and punishments. Unlike adult courts, there are no juries in juvenile courts. A judge decides the verdict and necessary punishment for a juvenile offender. Most

A group of young offenders awaits the next activity of the day at a juvenile detention facility.

juveniles are not sent to prisons if they have been found guilty of a crime. Instead, they are normally held in a juvenile detention center, also know as "juvie."

Incarceration for the young is very different than imprisonment for adults. Some facilities resemble home environments and focus on education and rehabilitation. Juvenile records are often erased or sealed once offenders have served their sentence.

According to the U.S. Department of Justice, there are fewer young people in juvenile facilities today than there were in 1997. However, there are more young people serving time in adult prison than ever before. Today, almost all states have laws that allow offenders under the age of eighteen to be prosecuted as adults if they commit a crime like robbery or murder. Placing children in adult prisons may lower the number of children in juvenile detention, but the long-term effects may be very damaging. Juvenile offenders are often abused and fare very badly in the general prison population. In addition, without the education and counseling that detention centers provide, juveniles serving time in adult prisons are at a great disadvantage.

Women in Prison

The number of women in prison across the United States is on the rise. Department of Justice statistics tell us that this number has increased ten-fold in the past twenty years. Many of these women have been imprisoned as a result of the tougher drug laws passed in the 1980s and 1990s. In New York, for example, the live-in girlfriend of a drug dealer is considered just as guilty as the dealer, and she can receive as many as fifteen years in prison for a first offense.

Women in prison have the added burden of being guarded by both men and women. According to Amnesty International, an organization that is dedicated to protecting the rights of human beings around the world, inmates in women's prisons are abused verbally, physically, and even sexually by male guards. In some cases, guards have threatened inmates' visitation rights and other privileges if female inmates were to file complaints against them.

Families suffer when the number of imprisoned women increases. Seventy percent of female inmates have at least one child, according to a 2000 *Time* magazine article. What happens to these children? Some stay with relatives while mothers serve their time. But some single mothers with no family must watch helplessly as the state sends their children into foster care until they are released. Visiting mothers in prison is difficult for children. Many prisons are located in areas that are hard to reach, and the environment may be threatening and very foreign.

Gangs

Prison gangs pose a large problem in penitentiaries throughout America. In fact, many gangs were begun in prisons in order to protect inmates from violence. In addition to the rules set by prison staff, gangs often have their own codes of conduct, as well as their own brand of violent justice.

Gangs and tight-knit prison groups use tattoos to identify members. For this reason and others, most prisons outlaw tattooing, which is done with improvised tattooing equipment. Gangs also use secret hand signals and other ways of identifying one another.

Inside prisons, gangs can control the flow of contraband and illegal substances, such as drugs, alcohol, and cigarettes. (Tobacco use is permitted in some prisons, but as of 2002, at least thirty-eight of fifty state correctional departments were either smoke-free or had partial smoking bans.) Gangs can also have an influence on the

Police officers lift a gang member's shirt to reveal his identifying body art. Inside and outside prison walls, many gangs use unique tattoos to show membership.

world outside of prisons. Inmates who join gangs while in prison may be called upon after they are released to perform illegal tasks outside of prison or to help smuggle money or drugs back and forth.

Race

As in society in general, race is a difficult issue in American prisons. Many critics claim that U.S. laws and law enforcement are biased against people of color, resulting in more minorities behind bars. According to the Department of Justice, 1 in 106 white male adults was behind bars at the beginning of 2008. Compare this to 1 in 36 Hispanic males and 1 in 15 black males.

Inmates of one race often separate themselves from other races. New inmates (called "fish" by longtime inmates) may feel pressure to join a gang for protection from gangs of other races. As a result, interracial and interethnic hatred continues.

Prisons themselves often promote this racial separation. In California, for example, state prisons place new inmates in cells with inmates of the same race or background for the first two months of their sentence. The goal of the policy is to stop gang violence, but it also serves to increase anger and reduce trust among inmates of different ethnicities. Of course, prison overcrowding makes racial tensions worse.

Violence, Riots, and Abuse

Violence between inmates is common in U.S. prisons. In addition, violence by inmates directed at corrections and prison staff is a problem. At the most extreme level, this sort of violence leads to rioting, hostage taking, and death. For example, in 2007, five hundred prisoners at a medium-security facility in Indiana rose up to protest their treatment. The riot left two guards and seven inmates injured and caused thousands of dollars in fire damage. Correctional officers are known to commit acts of violence against inmates, too. For example, in August 2007, a corrections officer named Ryan Michael Teel was sentenced for abusing inmates at the Harrison County Adult Detention Center in Gulfport, Mississippi. Teel was found guilty in the beating death of inmate Jessie Lee Williams Jr. A broader investigation into Williams's death resulted in the arrest of eight corrections officers. They pled guilty to crimes involving civil rights violations.

Mental Health and Medical Care

In November 2000, a group of guards at Cedar Junction, a Massachusetts correctional institution, was authorized to tie down inmate Hakeem Obba. Over four days, he was kept in shackles for more than forty hours. Obba had had more than two hundred citations for disruptive behavior, including stabbing an officer and smearing feces on his cell walls. Sadly, he committed suicide two months later. His behavior should have alerted prison staff to perform a mental health evaluation, which may have saved his life.

Mental illness like that of inmate Hakeem Obba is not a rarity in prisons. Rates of mental illness and suicide in inmate populations are three times as high as they are in the general population. And 1 in every 6 inmates is suffering from some sort of mental illness. According to a 2003 report by Human Rights Watch, the illnesses include bipolar disorder and schizophrenia, which usually require medication to control. Inmates with severe disorders like these have the potential to make prison even more dangerous by hurting themselves and others. Mentally ill prisoners may also have great difficulty obeying the strict rules of daily prison life, which can result in punishments that they may have difficulty accepting.

In general, the quality of mental health treatment has improved in prisons over the last ten years, but there is still much improvement to be made. Corrections officers are not always properly trained to diagnose or treat inmates with mental health issues, and they should not be expected to do so. That job should be left to mental health professionals. However, as many state and federal mental hospitals have closed due to shrinking budgets, the burden of treating mentally ill inmates is increasingly shifting to prison administrators and staff.

Privatization

Longer sentences, stricter drug laws, and the elimination of parole in some states all contribute to the current overcrowding in American prisons. Overcrowding in prisons has caused many states to turn to private

Prison inmates perform work for a private company. The work can vary from answering phones to assembling mechanical parts.

companies in order to ease the burden. Privatization is not a new concept. Private companies have supplied medical care and other services to government facilities for many years. However, after the 1980s, prison over-crowding became severe enough that states began to allow more nongovernment companies to run prisons. Some companies took over state prisons, while others built new facilities to house inmates.

Private prisons make money by charging state governments for each person they incarcerate. Private companies mainly run minimum- and medium-security prisons. Supporters of prison privatization argue that federal and state governments pay less money to prisons that are private than they would if the prisons were government-run. Another benefit of privatization, supporters say, is competition. If many companies are competing to manage prisons, then this gives local, state, and federal governments the opportunity to choose the best one available.

One of the main arguments against privatization is that private prison companies do not have to answer to a higher authority, as do prisons run by state or federal governments. Other critics say that corporations shouldn't be involved in hospitals, prisons, and other institutions that serve the whole of a nation. The goal of corporations is to maximize profits. Critics fear that the desire for profits leads private prisons to economize when it comes to safety, training, aid for the mentally ill and for other prison programs. Therefore, cutting corners puts both workers and inmates in greater danger.

The opening of private prisons has slowed over the last ten years, and some have closed. Still, according to a 2008 report by Global Research, there were more than one hundred private correctional centers and prisons across the United States housing more than 62,000 inmates.

Americans have a choice in deciding the future of incarceration in our country. Changes can be made in corrections spending and sentencing laws to improve prison conditions. Corrections officers and prison staff can be better trained and equipped, and inmate rehabilitation and education can be made more useful.

Smarter Budgets

Billions of dollars are spent each year to keep Americans in prison. Of course, prisons are needed to protect citizens from violent criminals. However, some states and citizens are wondering if so much spending on nonviolent criminals merely takes money away from other important programs. Legislation like California's Proposition 36 may provide answers.

Passed in 2000, Proposition 36 allows treatment to be an option for first- and second-time drug possession, instead of prison. (Proposition 36 does not apply to

These drug offenders shorten their sentences by agreeing to six months of military-style training along with drug treatment. This will also save taxpayers money.

violent offenders.) From 2000 to 2006, Proposition 36 saved California taxpayers more than $1 billion.

In 2007, the U.S. Supreme Court ruled that federal judges may, at their discretion, reduce mandatory minimum sentences for crack cocaine possession. This decision could result in early release for almost 20,000 federal inmates in prison under the previous federal mandatory minimum sentence of nineteen years.

Better Training

Corrections programs are constantly looking for ways to improve prisons. For example, the Commission on Abuse and Safety in America's Prisons spent 2005 looking at the most serious problems inside correctional facilities. The commission found that one of the hardest issues to address was the tremendous burden placed on the men and women who staff our country's prisons, many times without adequate leadership, training, or resources.

Correctional officers and wardens from around the United States were interviewed by the commission about their most serious challenges. One officer described being ordered by superiors to beat an inmate. Others complained of inadequate training and low pay for such a dangerous job. A prison administrator complained that his correctional officers are expected to be able to deal with young inmates, old inmates, and both men and women. In addition, he noted, officers have to be aware of emotionally unstable, suicidal, or violent inmates. And if that weren't enough, officers may find their lives endangered if they fail to recognize gang activity, or if they do not speak foreign languages.

In the end, the commission emphasized the need to keep these issues at the forefront of a national discussion about prisons and prison life.

Skills for the Outside

Assisting people once they are released from prison is crucial to prison reform. Teaching usable skills in prison can help to ensure that a greater number of former inmates do not return to prison. With the strict schedules of prisons behind them, many of those released are unsure of how to fill their days, and they often have trouble finding work. Some employers are unwilling to hire men and women who have served prison time, so unemployment for former inmates is much higher than for the general population.

Conclusion

There is much work to be done if our prisons are to be places where inmates can be treated fairly and educated for life outside as they repay their debt to society. No single law or change can solve the problems facing prisons in the United States today. Yet, policy makers are more aware than ever that some offenders need prison sentences, while others can be safely handled in the community.

Raising education standards, reducing poverty, and creating jobs are just a few social reforms that can ultimately serve to keep more of our citizens out of prison. The problems of our prisons are not being ignored, but solving large problems takes consideration and time before results can be seen. Ultimately, the issues discussed in this book are connected, and making progress in one area can lead to progress all around.

Glossary

advocate Person who pleads the cause or case of another.

confinement State of being jailed or locked away.

contraband Prohibited or illegal items.

ethnicity Classification of people according to race or nationality.

incapacitation To disable or prevent a person from moving or acting.

incarceration To put in prison.

juvenile Young person in the years before adulthood.

minimum sentencing When a judge must deliver a fixed sentence to anyone convicted of a particular crime.

penitentiary Prison or jail.

privatization Making a business or system private, rather than public.

privilege Right defined by a person's place in an organization.

probation Time during which a convicted offender's sentence is suspended; if the terms are broken, then a penalty will result.

recidivism Return to previous bad or criminal behavior.

rehabilitation Process of correcting bad behavior or qualities.

warden Supervisor of a jail or prison.

For More Information

Federal Bureau of Prisons
320 First Street NW
Washington, DC 20534
(202) 307-3198
Web site: http://www.bop.gov
The Federal Bureau of Prisons protects public safety by ensuring that federal offenders serve their sentences in facilities that are safe, humane, cost-efficient, and appropriately secure.

National Citizens United for Rehabilitation of Errants (National CURE)
P.O. Box 2310
Washington, DC 20013-2310
(202) 789-2126
Web site: http://www.curenational.org
CURE's members all share the view that the criminal justice system must improve.

National Gang Crime Research Center
P.O. Box 990
Peotone, IL 60468-0990
(708) 258-9111
Web site: http://www.ngcrc.com

This nonprofit, independent agency promotes research on gangs, gang members, and gang problems in cooperation with federal, state, and local government agencies.

National Institute of Corrections
320 First Street NW
Washington, DC 20534
(800) 995-20534
(202) 307-3106
Web site: http://www.nicic.org
The National Institute of Corrections is an agency within the U.S. Department of Justice, Federal Bureau of Prisons, which provides training, technical assistance, information services, and policy and program development assistance to federal, state, and local corrections agencies.

Web Sites

Due to the changing nature of Internet links, Rosen Publishing has developed an online list of Web sites related to the subject of this book. This site is updated regularly. Please use this link to access the list:

http://www.rosenlinks.com/itn/inca

For Further Reading

Castle Rock Entertainment. *The Shawshank Redemption* (1994). (Film)

Esherick, Joan. *Women in Prison*. Broomall, PA: Mason Crest, 2006.

Herival, Tara, and Paul Wright, eds. *Prison Profiteers: Who Makes Money from Mass Incarceration*. New York, NY: New Press, 2009.

Libal, Autumn. *The Social, Monetary, and Moral Costs of Prisons*. Broomall, PA: Mason Crest, 2006.

Martin, Tom. *Behind Prison Walls: The Real World of Working in Today's Prisons*. Boulder, CO: Paladin Press, 2003.

National Geographic Channel. *Prison Nation* (2007). (Television program)

Russell, Craig. *Alternatives to Prison*. Broomall, PA: Mason Crest, 2006.

Smith, Roger. *The History of Incarceration*. Broomall, PA: Mason Crest, 2006.

Talvi, Silja J. A. *Women Behind Bars: The Crisis of Women in the U.S. Prison System*. Berkeley, CA: Seal Press, 2007.

Bibliography

Anti-Defamation League. "Bigotry Behind Bars:
    Racist Groups in U.S. Prisons." Retrieved August 19,
    2008 (http://www.adl.org/presrele/asus_12/
    3291_12.asp).

Commission on Safety and Abuse in America's Prisons.
    "Corrections Officers Describe a Difficult, Stressful
    Job and Conditions That Put Staff and Prisoners at
    Risk." November 1, 2005. Retrieved October 22, 2008
    (http://www.prisoncommission.org/press_release_
    110105.asp).

Cosgrove-Mather, Bootie. "Smuggling Drugs into the
    Slammer: Illegal Drugs Regularly Make It to Federal
    Prisoners." CBS News, January 23, 2003. Retrieved
    September 1, 2008 (http://www.cbsnews.com/stories/
    2003/01/23/national/main537650.shtml).

David, Ruth. "Ten Alternatives to Prison." *Forbes*, April 18,
    2006. Retrieved August 15, 2008 (http://www.forbes.
    com/2006/04/15/prison-justice-alternatives_cx_rd_
    06slate_0418alter.html).

Foucalt, Michel, and Alan Sheridan. *Discipline and Punish:
    The Birth of the Prison*. New York, NY: Vintage
    Books, 1995.

Gibbons, John J., and Nicholas de B. Katzenbach.
    Confronting Confinement: A Report of the

Commission on Safety and Abuse in America's Prisons. New York, NY: Vera Institute of Justice, 2006.

Hales, Larry. "U.S. Prison Population Explodes." *World Peace Diet*, March 10, 2008. Retrieved August 8, 2008 (http://www.worldpeacediet.com/2008/03/ us-prison-popul.html).

Hawkins, Gordon J. *The Prison: Policy and Practice.* Chicago, IL: University of Chicago Press, 1982.

Human Rights Watch. *Ill-Equipped: U.S. Prisons and Offenders with Mental Illness.* New York, NY: Human Rights Watch, 2003.

Lin, Ann Chih. *Reform in the Making: The Implementation of Social Policy in Prison.* Princeton, NJ: Princeton University Press, 2002.

Liptak, Adam. "Inmate Count in U.S. Dwarfs Other Nations." *New York Times*, April 23, 2008. Retrieved October 22, 2008 (http://www.nytimes.com/2008/04/ 23/us/23prison.html).

Morris, Norval, and David J. Rothman. *The Oxford History of the Prison: The Practice of Punishment in Western Society.* New York, NY: Oxford University Press, 1997.

Selcraig, Bruce. "Camp Fear." *Mother Jones*, November/ December 2000. Retrieved September 1, 2008 (http://www.motherjones.com/news/feature/2000/11/ campfear.html).

Springer, Dan. "An Alternative to Jail: Inmates Work Off Fines." *La Crosse Tribune*, May 19, 2008. Retrieved October 22, 2008 (http://www.lacrossetribune.com/articles/2008/05/19/news/00lead.txt).

Tuhus-Dubrow, Rebecca. "Women in Prison." *The Nation*, March 25, 2004. Retrieved September 1, 2008 (http://www.thenation.com/doc/20040412/tuhusdubrow).

USA Today. "Indiana Prison Riot Quelled." May 25, 2007. Retrieved October 22, 2008 (http://www.usatoday.com/news/nation/2007-04-24-prison-riot_N.htm).

U.S. Department of Justice. "Summary Findings." 2007. Retrieved August 19, 2008 (http://www.ofp.usdoj.gov/bjs/prisons.htm).

Warren, Jennifer. *One in 100: Behind Bars in America 2008*. Pew Center on the States. Retrieved August 20, 2008 (http://www.pewcenteronthestates.org/report_detail.aspx?id=35904).

Index

About the Author

Kerry Hinton lives in Brooklyn, New York. He has family members who counsel prison inmates, and he has had an interest in criminal justice since he served as a command legal officer in the U.S. Navy.

Photo Credits

Cover (top left) © www.istockphoto.com/Eliza Snow; cover (top right) © Jonathan Allain; cover (bottom), p. 37 © Justin Sullivan/Getty Images; p. 4 © www.istockphoto.com/Andrejs Zemdega; p. 8 © Erich Lessing/Art Resource; p. 12 © Robert King/Newsmakers/Getty Images; p. 14 © Todd Plitt/Getty Images; p. 15 © www.istockphoto.com/Monique Rodriguez; pp. 16, 23, 36 Federal Bureau of Prisons; p. 19 © Davis Turner-Pool/Getty Images; p. 21 Federal Bureau of Prisons/Getty Images: p. 25 © www.istockphoto.com/Todd Bates; pp. 26, 30, 42, 49, 52 © AP Photos; pp. 33, 38 © Scott Olson/Getty Images; p. 35 © Bettmann/Corbis; p. 45 © Robert Nicklesberg/Getty Images; p. 51 © www.istockphoto.com/Stephen Newman.

Designer: Tom Forget; Editor: Christopher Roberts
Photo Researcher: Marty Levick